Are You More Like......?

Chris Cavert, M.S.

Susana Acosta, M.A.

Published by:

Wood & Barnes Publishing
2717 NW 50th
Oklahoma City, OK 73112
(405) 942-6812

1st Edition © 2002, Chris Cavert.
All rights reserved.

Printed in the United States of America
Oklahoma City, Oklahoma
ISBN # 1885473419

Cover art by Blue Design.
Copy editing/design by Canela Winstead.

To order copies of this book, please call:
Jean Barnes Books
800-678-0621

Aknowledgements

We give our utmost thanks to Mary Sue Cavert and Susana's advisory & kids for their fun contributions. And as always, to the wonderful support and effort put in by the Wood 'N' Barnes Publishing staff.

Activity Idea from:
"Games (and other stuff) for Teachers"

Procedure: Clear out the center of the room as much as possible and form a nice big circle with your group.

You will ask the players to choose one of the two characteristics from each statement you are going to read. If they are more like the first characteristic, have them step inside the circle. If they are more like the second characteristic, have them stay where they are as part of the circle. Leave a little time between each statement to give the students a chance to see who else is standing with them. Play along with them, by just stepping in and out of the circle as you read.

That's the simple gist. We like to use this activity as our introduction to the process of active learning (getting up and moving around). We keep it simple the first time with a little processing after. Down the road we can use this activity again to bring out more personal perspectives and discussions.

Introduction

The first couple of hundred "Are You More Like...." questions appeared in the book, "Games (and other stuff) for Teachers" by Chris Cavert and Laurie Frank. We had such a great response to the first set of questions and had so much fun thinking of them, we just couldn't stop there. The latest Pocket Prompter has 1001 "Are You More Like..." ponderables that can help open up discussions to many different topics. While you've got your group pondering keep in mind the questions are also useful for personality identification and like/dislike elimination. This book is also a useful ice breaking tool for groups of any age.

You will have a great deal of fun with these questions. When using them, try to encourage the participants to think more about the characteristics of the items. Younger groups will often just choose the item they like best-nothing wrong with that! Do whatever works best for your group. Because this book was created for such a wide variety of audiences we have bold typed the questions that may be more effective for older participants or produce more complex thought. Feel free to add your own ideas. Just don't forget to keep the spirit of fun in all that you do.

Are You
More Like...

wacky or weird?

noon or midnight?

a flower or a weed?

Are You More Like......

a gallery or a museum?

a crossword puzzle or a word search?

a bloom or a bud?

hard boiled or scrambled eggs?

the coffee table or the kitchen table?

insatiable or satisfied?

a slide or a swing?

head lights or tail lights?

a trick or a treat?

a stander or a sitter?

a pink flamingo or a lawn gnome?

express or standard?

auditory or visual?

an action or a reaction?

a yo-yo or a spinning top?

a country farm or a neighborhood?

Are You More Like......

a ladder or a pole?

the ocean or the mountains?

a bracelet, a necklace, or a ring?

cash or a gift certificate?

figure skating or speed skating?

aluminum or wood?

black or white?

a lemon or a lime?

the mast or the rudder?

the escalator or the stairs?

up front or out back?

a sponge or a strainer?

imminent or possible?

cardboard or paper?

a cat or a dog?

calm or hyper?

a hot tub or a sauna?

the United States or a foreign country?

evaporation or solidification?

A's or B's?

Are You More Like......

fur or scales?

a country or a state?

an almanac or a biography?

the defense or the offense?

a cause or an effect?

spots or stripes?

Ballet or Hip-Hop?

a fountain or a waterfall?

influential or listless?

a bottle or a can?

a small group or a large group?

touch, smell, taste, sight or sound?

Tupperware© or Ziplocks©?

mass or space?

a dictionary or a thesaurus?

a night shirt or a knight's suit of armor?

mind or matter?

an explorer or a settler?

boxers or briefs?

flats or high heels?

Are You More Like......

extraordinary or normal?

"a change of pace" or
                    "the same old same old"?

the roots or the limbs?

a cable or a clamp?

nutricious or delicious?

a passenger or a pilot?

sunshine or moon light?

Shakespeare or Dr. Suess?

an aisle or a window seat?

a kaleidoscope or a telescope?

the cheese or the macaroni?

the table of contents or the index?

a hard cover book or a paperback book?

the desert or the rain forest?

the arrow or the target?

a door or a window?

a China cabinet or a trophy case?

to be or not to be?

a bird's song or a frog's croak?

heads or tails?

Are You More Like......

the landing or the take-off?

a bun or a loaf?

married or single?

an animal lover or a people lover?

energy or calm?

an M.V.P. or a V.I.P.?
(Most Valuable Player or Very Important Person)

a drawing or a painting?

a paramedic or a police officer?

a nine iron or a putter?

the fixture or the light?

a buyer or a maker?

the front porch or the back porch?

fleece or leather?

clockwise or counterclockwise?

Are You More Like......

an arrival or a departure?

a café or a deli?

air waves or wires?

please or thank you?

a TV dinner or fast food?

by the clock or by the moment?

Are You More Like......

an apartment or a house?

liquid soap or powdered soap?

a coat or a vest?

a coconut or a pineapple?

the kitchen or the living room?

in or out?

the door or the doorknob?

the ball or the chain?

a ball or a strike?

economy or luxury?

a cold shower or a hot shower?

a sitcom or a drama?

a giver or a receiver?

a boomerang or a Frisbee©?

inflated or reduced?

a magazine or a newspaper?

a candle or a flashlight?

a trash can or a recycling bin?

a movie or prime time?

an address or a phone number?

Are You More Like......

the ugly duckling or the swan?

socks or shoes?

"enough is enough" or "grin and bear it"?

the Equator or the North Pole?

plain or peanut?

a garden or a playground?

french toast or pancakes?

a carpenter or a plumber?

a carport or a garage?

ground beef or a T-bone?

a fruit or a vegetable?

a copy or an original?

an air conditioner or a furnace?

air mail or an E-mail?

Are You More Like......

a carpet or a rug?

anything or something?

rock, paper or scissors?

a fan or a vacuum cleaner?

a story or a song?

shy or cautious?

Are You More Like......

baking or grilling?

Battleship© or Tic Tac Toe©?

a cough or a sneeze?

a kite or a sailboat?

East or West?

Biology or Geology?

a country road or the highway?

a trickster or a truth teller?

loud or quiet?

a mover or a shaker?

the center or the edge?

a museum or a circus?

an adjustment or a revision?

place mats or a table cloth?

an expert or novice?

a plain cone or waffle cone?

the green or the rough?

a chalkboard or a dry erase board?

a guest or a host?

the cup or the saucer?

Are You More Like......

traditional or contemporary?

a bagel or a slice of bread?

shoes or socks?

full service or self service?

a Bell Boy or a Bus Boy?

affordable or expensive?

a daisy or a rose?

listening or reading?

the Empire State Building or
          the Great Wall of China?

a catcher or a pitcher?

lobster or shrimp?

excited or reserved?

an oven or a refrigerator?

action or suspense?

Are You More Like......

a cushion or a pillow?

art or music?

punt, pass or kick?

the land or the sea?

aluminum foil or plastic wrap?

the commuter train or the HOV lane?

Are You More Like......

a paint gun or a water gun?

chocolate or strawberries?

an egineer or a mechanic?

American or Swiss cheese?

consensus or majority?

the hider or the seeker?

an amusement park or a water park?

rain water or well water?

fireworks or a laser show?

rapids or ripples?

a bath or a shower?

diet or regular?

a reaction or a response?

a hill or a mountain?

a window or a mirror?

honey or sugar?

a student or a teacher?

a box fan or a ceiling fan?

a honey bee or a bumble bee?

a jump or a dive?

Are You More Like......

a gift-bag or gift wrap?

the young or the old?

an event or a mediation?

a jukebox or a music box?

a belcher or a passer?

a taco or a tamale?

a hand written or typed letter?

stern or lenient?

the outdoors or the indoors?

a cruise or an expedition?

a bikini or a one piece?

an opera or a rodeo?

a dollar or a penny?

a private school or public school?

a cherry or a lemon?

accidental or intentional?

a moon or a star?

a ferris wheel or a merry-go-round?

a broom or a vacuum?

a field or a forest?

Are You More Like.......

a pickup truck or a van?

letters or numbers?

delayed or en route?

a bubble bath or mineral bath?

a wish or an idea?

a mountain climber or a spelunker?

simple or complicated?

the book cover or book pages?

a pier or a raft?

conform or differ?

wheat or white bread?

an ax or a chainsaw?

cheesecake or Jello®?

the inside or the outside?

Baby blue or Navy blue?

scientific or theological?

freedom or slavery?

a screen door or wooden door?

a blimp or a submarine?

drifting or steering?

Are You More Like......

a signature or a seal?

jacks or marbles?

a convertible or a minivan?

a jester or a king?

abbreviated or expanded?

a buyer or a seller?

jelly or peanut butter?

the washer or the dryer?

a bedroom or a loft?

check in or carry on?

everybody or somebody?

Karate or Thai Chi?

Bluegrass or Opera?

a preacher or a teacher?

Are You More Like.......

a hot springs or a Jacuzzi©?

humble or proud?

the library or a bookstore?

brave or afraid?

Bob Cratchet or Mr. Scrooge?

pasta or rice?

Are You More Like.......

an ear or an eye?

an order or a request?

an alien or a native?

coffee or tea?

an organ or a piano?

the forest or a tree?

a camping chair or a hammock?

a forward or a goalie?

potato chips or pretzels?

art or mathematics?

doubles or singles?

England or Australia?

an experience or a metaphor?

a paintbrush or a roller?

a banner or a flag?

deodorant or antiperspirant?

racquet ball or tennis?

crayons or paint?

adding or subtracting?

a best seller book or a second hand book?

Are You More Like......

a desktop or a laptop computer?

stars or stripes?

barrel racing or bull riding?

a stander or a leaner?

multiple choice questions or an essay?

Los Angeles or New York?

the bowling ball or the bowling pin?

an eraser or White-Out©?

stocks or mutual funds?

a card or a note?

the cucumber or the pickle?

a lighter or a match?

a shopper or a sightseer?

a witness or a victim?

Are you More Like......

a lighthouse or an outhouse?

even or irregular?

"Out of the blue" or "Out in the open"?

a cloth napkin or paper napkins?

"An eye for an eye" or
              "Turn the other cheek?"

lined or unlined paper?

Are You More Like.......

brakes or downshifting?

off or on?

a hotel or a motel?

patient or restless?

a tourist or a resident?

a grin or a laugh?

"break even" or "go for broke"?

a pocket watch or a wrist watch?

exceed or lag?

salt or pepper?

depth or width?

country music or rap music?

peppermint or cinnamon?

the basement or the attic?

catsup or mustard?

a gas fireplace or wood-burning fireplace?

salt or sugar?

a ball cap or a visor?

an editor or a writer?

an egg timer or an hour glass?

Are You More Like......

automatic or manual transmission?

a picnic or a restaurant?

a happy birthday or a Happy New Year?

down or up?

sandals or tennis shoes?

a clothing store or a toy store?

an amateur or a veteran?

blackjack or the slot machines?

downtown or uptown?

masking tape or scotch tape?

roller blades or roller skates?

Twister© or Scrabble©?

a highlight or an underline?

Velcro©or zippers?

buttered or plain popcorn?

an explanation or a complication?

a vendor or a vending machine?

meatballs or spaghetti?

dirt or grass?

a meeting or a memo?

Are You More Like.......

love or labor?

change or consistency?

mental or physical?

the exterior or the interior?

a boy or a man?

a corporate executive or an entrepreneur?

a fog horn or a light house?

a millionaire or a pauper?

cable or satellite?

blended or stirred?

lip gloss or lip stick?

passive or active?

a choice or a chance?

Big Bird® or Oscar the Grouch®?

cake or cookies?

rope or thread?

the favorite or the underdog?

polo or water polo?

bald or a full head of hair?

a song or a dance?

Are You More Like......

a pop-up toaster or a toaster oven?

a hard hat or a top hat?

a burger or fried chicken?

the tortoise or the hare?

a Speedo© or trunks?

a belt or suspenders?

exempt or responsible?

gel or mousse?

bubble gum or chewing gum?

a sand trap or a water hazard?

boots or sandals?

an elf or a giant?

stain or varnish?

downhill or slalom skiing?

staying at home or going on vacation?

the bottom or the top?

endless or fixed?

the mud or the sand?

the bow or the arrow?

right brained or left brained?

Are You More Like.......

fishing or hunting?

summers on the beach or winter in the Alps?

a cap or a hat?

international or national?

wacky or weird?

a note or a recording?

the driver or a passenger?

noon or midnight?

an agreement or a debate?

a clock or a wrist watch?

North or South?

a flower or a weed?

a cab or limousine?

a corner or a side?

a follower or a leader?

a mobile phone or a public phone?

carpet or a wooden floor?

"A" or "Z"?

the monkey bars or the swing set?

unique or usual?

Are You More Like......

a comment or a suggestion?

the Grand Canyon or Pike's Peak?

carry out or delivery?

skim milk or 2%?

a foot or a meter?

a patch work quilt or a stain glass window?

billiards or pinball?

a donkey or a horse?

a garage sale or storage?

drive in or a drive through?

coins or paper money?

the infield or the outfield?

a 35 millimeter camera or a Polaroid?

a bird or a fish?

far or near?

loose leaf or spiral bound paper?

a bumper or a fender?

a square nut or a wing nut?

a bulldozer or a crane?

"hello" or "good-bye"?

Are You More Like......

trash or treasure?

half empty or half full?

a barbershop or a salon?

a bus or a cab?

expectant or indifferent?

an Opera or a pantomime?

a bus trip or a plane ride?

absorbent or impervious?

lease or own?

comfortable or uneasy?

full price or on special?

french fries or onion rings?

"In the dark" or "In the great wide open"?

parking near the door or away from the door?

an essay or a poem?

a term paper or a project?

an answering machine or caller ID?

cookies or rice cakes?

a paper clip or a rubber band?

the fruit or the vine?

Are You More Like.......

a cardboard box or a plastic container?

jump rope or hopscotch?

a wheel chair or a cane?

an oak or a willow tree?

checkers or chess?

together or apart?

oil or vinegar?

an obstacle or an assistance?

a visitor or a local?

an athelete or a genius?

a castle or a cottage?

the sneak preview or the video?

the future or the past?

a soak or a spin?

skin or bones?

earmuffs or a hat?

soda or water?

a knight or a peasant?

a country club or a night club?

a ladybug or a praying mantis?

Are You More Like......

dinner or supper?

a story book reader or a story teller?

a field or a stream?

a principal or a teacher?

a dot.com or a dot.org?

the train or the track?

a can or a jar?

a finger or a thumb?

morning, noon, or night?

an exit ramp or an on ramp?

biased or fair?

sugar or artificial sweetner?

a fire-cracker or a sparkler?

a photo album or a picture frame?

canines or molars?

an advance or a retreat?

a massage or a whirlpool?

an adverb or a verb?

a clap or a snap?

grass or sand?

Are You More Like.......

an advisor or an encourager?

a planter or a vase?

an export or an import?

work or play?

the back yard or the playground?

a cup or a gallon?

a player or a spectator?

a gulper or a sipper?

a chapter book or a picture book?

a doctor or a nurse?

hamburgers or hotdogs?

the pass or the run?

a cloudy or sunny day?

a baked potato or french-fries?

once or twice?

habitual or sporadic?

a phone call or a telegram?

Morse Code or sign language?

a checking or a savings account?

a tame or a wild horse?

Are You More Like......

a hanger or a hook?

a tarp or a tent?

Broadway or off-Broadway?

the exception or the rule?

a test or a quiz?

long sleeves or short sleeves?

the defendant or the plaintiff?

the long way home or a short cut?

shy or bold?

bubbles or a balloon?

the foundation or the structure?

ice cream or hot fudge?

concrete or wood?

a scientist or a artist?

the ceiling or the floor?

a four door or two door vehicle?

a doctor or a writer?

fingers or toes?

black & white or color?

a certainty or a quandary?

Are You More Like......

fragrant or odorless?

a raincoat or an umbrella?

a chain lock or a dead bolt?

a snow angel or snow man?

a new car or a used car?

an announcement or a secret?

man made or organic?

a hiking trail or a sidewalk?

an annoyance or a pleasure?

"Read between the lines" or "Say it like it is"?

the flame or the wax?

ready, willing or able?

The Beatles or Elvis?

disposable or rechargable batteries?

a rectangular table or a round table?

the hook or the line?

a closet or a trunk?

a doer or a thinker?

hand made or industrial?

a passing or a no-passing zone?

Are You More Like......

corn or wheat?

a believer or a skeptic?

singular or plural?

blunt or subtle?

a nature lover or a sports lover?

a tornado or an earthquake?

the club or the recreation center?

Cleopatra or Joan of Arc?

the President of the U.S. or John Doe?

an entry way or a closet?

designer or second hand?

the fence or the gate?

a bedroom or bathroom?

the moon or the sun?

Are you more like...   55

a door or a floor?

a morning person or night person?

abandoned or inhabited?

a campfire or a fireplace?

gas power or solar power?

"at the line" or "down the line"?

Are You More Like......

an electric blanket or a quilt?

an actor or a director?

a "Chip on your shoulder" or
a "Heart on your sleeve"?

glass or plastic?

an autobiography or a biography?

a 4 wheel drive or 2 wheel drive?

bottled water or tap water?

circles or lines?

mini-golf or 18 holes?

school or vacation?

a circle or a square?

the back or the front?

pants or shorts?

a backhand or forehand?

a cruise or a hike?

a "Jack of all trades" or a specialist?

the back seat or the front seat?

seasonal or year round?

friendly or antagonistic?

the shade or the sun?

Are You More Like......

blue or green?

the drums or the guitar?

shaken or stirred?

a journal or a tabloid?

a chord or a note?

a duffle bag or a suitcase?

hot sauce or mild sauce?

playing cards or trading cards?

a curl or a wave?

bells or whistles?

Romeo and Juliet or Star Wars©?

an open door or a closed door?

more or less?

a detective or a spy?

cotton or silk?

a Poodle or a Rotweiler?

the key or the lock?

a pen and ink drawing or a finger painting?

the original or the sequel?

ebb or flow?

Are You More Like......

a hawk or a vulture?

a bull or a bunny?

emotional or rational?

a bully or a nerd?

glue or tape?

a bun or a pony tail?

contacts or glasses?

a basket or shopping cart?

plaid or solids?

Africa or Antartica?

stop or yield?

a green light, a red light, or a yellow light?

a summary or "word-for-word"?

a burden or a breeze?

cupid or the tooth fairy?

a documentary or a safari?

a tree branch or a tree trunk?

skis or a snowboard?

cursive or printing?

A Capella or accompaniment?

Are You More Like......

a listener or a talker?

an acoustic or electric guitar?

a Picasso or a Renior?

exclusion or inclusion?

paid by the hour or paid by the job?

a slap stick or a stand up comic?

getting what you want or giving in?

a component or a system?

here or there?

candy or popcorn?

a critic or a fan?

a blanket or a sheet?

a ramp or a staircase?

a blink or a wink?

a wash or a wax?

a historical marker or a scenic overlook?

why or why not?

metric or standard?

a diver or a swimmer?

dull or sharp?

Are You More Like......

caffeinated or decaffeinated?

a sled or skis?

cutting or tearing?

A la Carte or an extra value meal?

a monopoly or an open market?

"All or nothing" or "Take what you can get"?

the post or the sign?

a fiddle or a violin?

infinite or limited?

an elevator or an escalator?

gloves or mittens?

an e-mail or a phone call?

an inner-tube or a raft?

a cassette tape or a CD?

a dialogue or a discussion?

a bow tie or a neck tie?

a scorpion or a snake?

a box or an envelope?

church or a night club?

jeans or khakis?

Are You More Like......

a gardener or a chef?

a nose ring or a toe ring?

dry goods or perishable?

"every day" or "every now and then"?

carry out or dine in?

King Arthur or Robin Hood?

a dolphin or a shark?

apples or oranges?

an optimist or a pessimist?

an aristocrat or a commoner?

a runner or a walker?

fork, knife or spoon?

a lake or a pool?

a glance or a look?

winning or losing?

a globe or a map?

a landlord or a tenant?

hot or cold cereal?

a drain or a vacuum?

a bush or a tree?

Are You More Like......

a stapler or a staple?

buttons or snaps?

a Michaelangelo or a Van Gogh?

a letter or a postcard?

family or company?

a canoe or a kayak?

even or odd?

a face lift or wrinkles?

cash or charge?

a time machine or a time capsule?

a dust cloth or a feather duster?

balancing or juggling?

a pen or a pencil?

the accelerator or the brakes?

a counter top or a shelf?

a ball or a bat?

solids or stripes?

the lawn or the garden?

a picker or a pickee?

a glider or a jet?

Are You More Like......

loose or tight?

a Mac or a PC?

a main course or a side dish?

combat boots or cowboy boots?

a campground or a rest stop?

a marker or a pen?

a manicure or a pedicure?

a chocolate chip cookie or an oatmeal cookie?

an exhale or an inhale?

a one-way trip or round trip?

enough or too much?

a paper clip or a staple?

the lottery or bingo?

a picnic blanket or picnic table?

an expiration or an inspiration?

a car or a truck?

for or against?

the median or the shoulder of the road?

a weekday or weekend?

chance or design?

Are You More Like......

an aid or an obstacle?

a playground or a stadium?

an extrovert or an introvert?

mild or spicy?

an airport or a bus station?

a map or a compass?

a clown or an acrobat?

the head lines or the bottom line?

a big screen or a compact screen?

Dr. Martin Luther King or Neil Armstrong?

exaggerated or underestimated?

a billboard or a bulletin board?

a poem or a story?

an alarm clock or a wake-up call?

a dam or a waterfall?

a microscope or a telescope?

Texas or Wisconsin?

hardware or software?

a Post-it Note©or a voicemail?

a book or television?

Are You More Like.......

a motor cross or a street racer?

the puzzle or the solution?

private or public?

an electric shaver or a razor?

a cave or a tree house?

radio or television?

a movie or a play?

order or confusion?

a farm or a ranch?

panicked or relaxed?

expected or surprised?

a chair or a couch?

happy or sad?

a bowl or a plate?

Are You More Like......

fish or steak?

a rocking chair or a wing back?

Ansel Adams or Leroy Neiman?

a No Trespassing sign or a Welcome mat?

a morning run or an afternoon stroll?

a climber or a digger?

Are You More Like......

an ant or a grasshopper?

recycle it or toss it?

flowering or hibernating?

an assistant or a rival?

an antonym or a synonym?

a full scale or a model?

expensive or free?

a dress shirt or a T-shirt?

a castle or a fortress?

work, rest, or play?

fair or foul?

body guard or a life guard?

the rose or the thorns?

an architect or a demolition man?

a donation or a grant?

a book or a book end?

a peacemaker or a troublemaker?

fussion or fission?

a sailor or a soldier?

a brown bag or a school lunch?

Are You More Like......

a one-way street or a two-way street?

a hearing aid or eyeglasses?

rain or shine?

a girl or a woman?

the chip or the dip?

a Greek tragedy or a science fiction novel?

pancakes or waffles?

credit or debit?

fire or ice?

a pillow or a rock?

a fireplace or a fountain?

city lights or stars?

an allusion or a specification?

a Butler or a Chauffeur?

a freeze or a thaw?

a clap or a whistle?

a backpack or a briefcase?

deliberate or spontaneous?

a talk show or a news report?

cooked or raw?

Are You More Like......

a bag or a box?

"Share the wealth" or "To each his/her own"?

a silouhette or a portrait?

a paper towel or a washcloth?

a bagel or a donut?

paper towels or a Kleenex©?

curly or straight?

the circus or the zoo?

custom made or factory direct?

the alarm or the snooze button?

fast or slow?

a brick or a stone?

snow skiing or water skiing?

a balcony or a porch?

early or late?

Broadway or Hollywood?

a perfectionist or easygoing?

leather or lace?

a spaceship or a submarine?

a camper or a tent?

Are You More Like......

overnight or standard ground?

astroturf or grass?

over the counter or prescription?

lotion or oil?

country pine or new car smell?

an artist or a patron?

pig out or work out?

a custom or a fad?

the fox or the hound?

a rainbow or a thunderstorm?

a frame or a picture?

the continuous line or dotted line on the road?

an advantage or a handicap?

a canoe or a jet ski?

a gradual grade or steep grade?

a conventional oven or a microwave?

a beach towel or a lounge chair?

plastic utensils or sterling silverware?

against the wind or with the wind?

a dash or a cup?

Are You More Like......

a bed or a sleeping bag?

the sunrise or the sunset?

gum or licorice?

a playhouse or a tree house?

baked or fried?

a ballad or rock 'n' roll?

a road or a straightaway?

ice cream or frozen yogurt?

in fashion or out of style?

a twist or a shout?

a foot or a hand?

Canada or Mexico?

a tank top or a T-shirt?

a billboard or a bumper sticker?

excellent or imperfect?

a camp or a country club?

lost or found?

long hair or short hair?

Thanksgiving or Valentine's day?

a cattle car or cattle drive?

Are You More Like.......

pictures or slides?

natural or florescent lighting?

a lecture or a party?

the problem or the solution?

dental floss or a toothpick?

adventurous or cautious?

AM or FM radio?

rain or snow?

a deposit or a withdrawal?

going or staying?

a saver or a spender?

a goose or a turkey?

criticism or flattery?

a week or a lifetime?

a chair or a table?

the high wire or the trapeze?

practical or theoretical?

a cruise ship or a yacht?

blocks or Legos©?

a reader or a writer?

Are You More Like......

an answer or a question?

a dishwasher or a hand washer?

blue or pink?

Winter, Spring, Summer, or Fall?

horizontal or vertical?

the next right or the next stop?

the beginning or the end?

a junkyard or a rose garden?

a dunk shot or a jump shot?

a bag clip or a twist tie?

an ice sculpture or a sand castle?

detergent or bleach?

"Full steam ahead" or
          "Take the long way home"?

casual or formal?

abstract or concrete?

bones or muscles?

feminine or masculine?

a caterpillar or a butterfly?

a dreamer or a realist?

the funny papers or the front page?

Are You More Like......

minor details or a general overview?

Peter Pan® or Wendy®?

a comic book or a history book?

a noun or a verb?

a tropical breeze or crisp mountain air?

awake or sleepy?

Saturday or Sunday?

downhill or uphill?

Hide-and-seek or "Lost and found"?

smart or stupid?

the high jump or the long jump?

diamonds or hearts?

back-to-back or face-to-face?

a clamp or a paper weight?

"In the cards" or "A sure thing"?

directory assistance (information) or
the phone book?

a shoe box or a shoe rack?

self service or a waiter?

a backpack or a duffle bag?

the drum or the stick?

Are You More Like.......

box seats or general admission?

a sun lover or a star gazer?

the judge or the jury?

a shield or a spear?

a blueberry or a raspberry?

line dry or tumble dry?

exactly or just about right?

abrupt or polite?

an only child or a sibling?

perishable or durable?

a hang glider or a parachute?

cheese or pepperoni pizza?

a buffet or menu item?

a bridge or a tunnel?

the force or the fulcrum?

the chicken or the egg?

going around or going through?

Outward Bound© or an urban adventure?

serious or funny?

a coloring book or a sketch book?

Are You More Like......

salted or unsalted?

electrical or manual?

a full room or an empty room?

active or idle?

an exercise bike or a treadmill?

bar soap or liquid soap?

stain remover or tiedye?

a steak or a salad?

ice or water?

a stalactite or a stalagmite?

sun screen or sun block?

a drawbridge or a moat?

the horse or the wagon?

a contract or a handshake?

left or right?

food or drinks?

a buyer or a trader?

stretching or weightlifting?

a beanbag chair or a Lazyboy©?

et cetera or period?

Are You More Like......

a bicycle or a tricycle?

common sense or a day dreamer?

the lightning or the thunder?

inseparable or divisible?

a life boat or a life jacket?

a miser or a philanthropist?

fact or fiction?

a bell or a buzzer?

a snake or a spider?

neccesary or optional?

right-side-up or up-side-down?

a roller coaster or a merry-go-round?

shingles or tiles?

sunny side up or sunny side over?

a tackle box or a tool box?

a hill or a valley?

a dog or a puppy?

forgiving or remembering?

a freckle or a dimple?

a bungee jump or a sky dive?

Are You More Like......

a mail box or a mail person?

play-by-play or uninterupted?

live or taped?

a wedding or a funeral?

furnished or unfurnished?

a talker or a thinker?

Mother Teresa or the Dalai Lama?

a nurse or a patient?

a note or a rest?

get over it or get with it?

homeade vanilla or
chocolate chip cookie dough ice cream?

a camillian or a gacko?

a chandelier or a candle?

a sparkler or a firecracker?

Are You More Like......

a puller or a pusher?

a guide dog or a guide book?

a referee or a player?

a refuge or a refugee?

yes or no?

Aspen, Colorado or Orlando, Florida?

Are You More Like......

a ditto or a question mark?

face-to-face or side-by-side?

paper or plastic?

the heart or the brain?

the jitter bug or the waltz?

........add your own!

About The Authors

Susana Acosta, M.A. has been a Spanish and English teacher for over twenty years. She has been recognized by her school as a Master Teacher and can be found in the 2002 edition of "Who's Who in American Teachers."

Susana was born in Madrid, Spain and stayed in school there until she received her Masters Degree in Art History from the University of Madrid. She has taught hundreds of children how to speak Spanish and English, has managed businesses, climbed mountains and traveled extensively. This is Susana's first publication but assuredly not her last.

Chris Cavert, M.S., has been active with groups of all ages for over 22 years. He is known around the United States as a trainer and speaker in the area of Adventure Based Activity Programming and focuses on how activities within this field help to develop and enhance pro-social behaviors, especially with youth populations.

Chris holds a Physical Education Teaching Degree from the University of Wisconsin-La Crosse and a Masters Degree in Experiential Education from Minnesota State University at Mankato, specializing in curriculum development.

Some of his first writing was published in the best selling *Chicken Soup for the Soul* series by Jack Canfield and Mark Victor Hansen. His activities have been published in books by Karl Rohnke, Sam Sikes, and Jim Cain. Since then Chris has written six books and co-authored three others. They include:

E.A.G.E.R. Curriculum
Affordable Portables
Games (and other stuff) for Group, Books 1& 2
Richochet and Other Fun Games With an Odd Ball
Games (and other stuff) for Teachers,
with Laurie Frank
50 Ways to Use Your Noodle: Loads of Land Games
with Foam Noodle Toys, with Sam Sikes
50 More Ways to Use Your Noodle: Loads of Land
Games with Foam Noodle Toys, with Sam Sikes
What Would it Be Like: 1001 Anytime Questions for
Anysize Answers

Chris' books focus on sharing activities that help educators, in many different fields, use experiential/adventure education to encourage pro-social behaviors in groups they work with.

For more information about Chris' publications and training opportunities, visit his site at:
www.fundoing.com.
To purchase any of his books, call Wood 'N' Barnes Publishing at 1-800-678-0621.

Are You More Like......